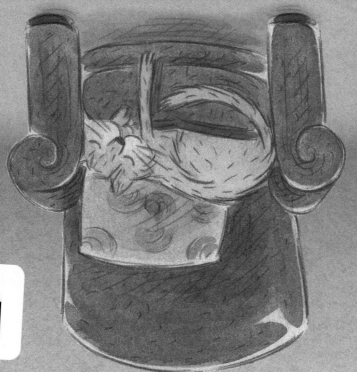

T03B6057

cat is sleeping

Written by Dee White
Illustrated by Tracie Grimwood

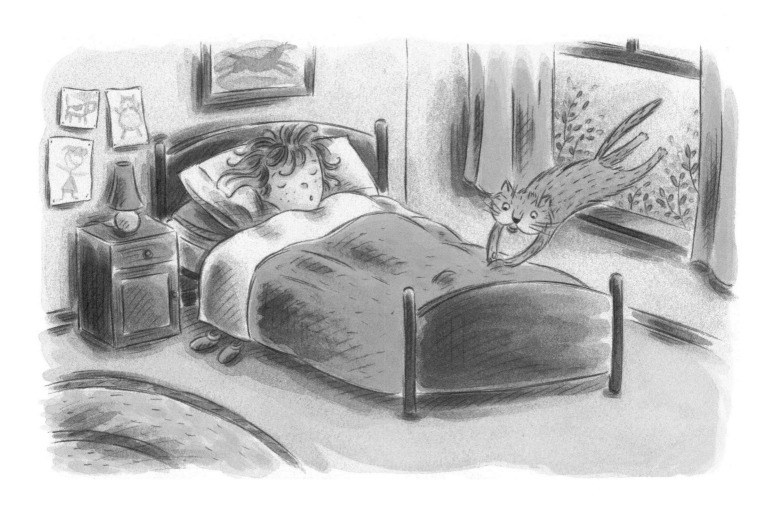

I am sleeping.

Cat is sleeping.

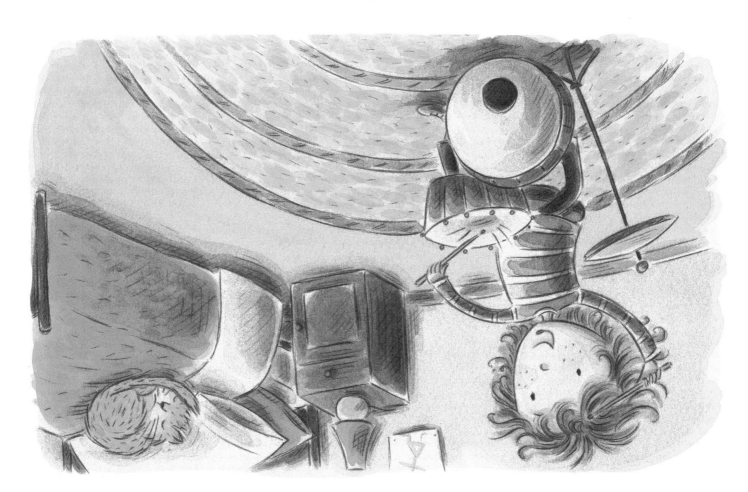

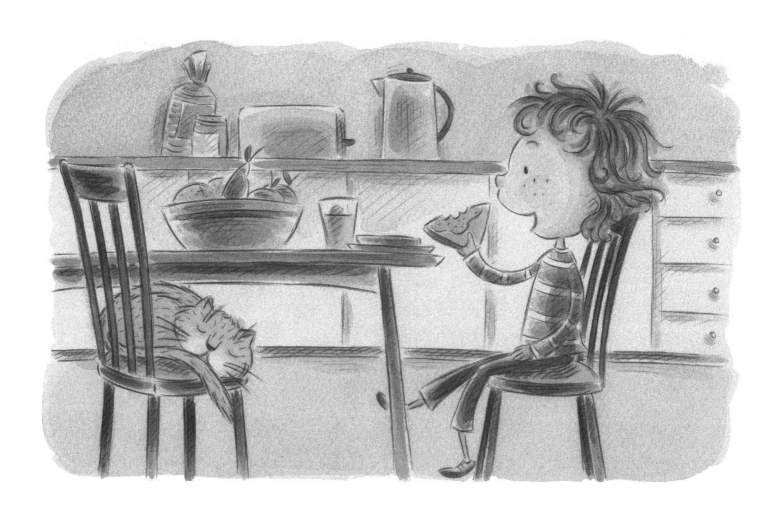

I am eating.

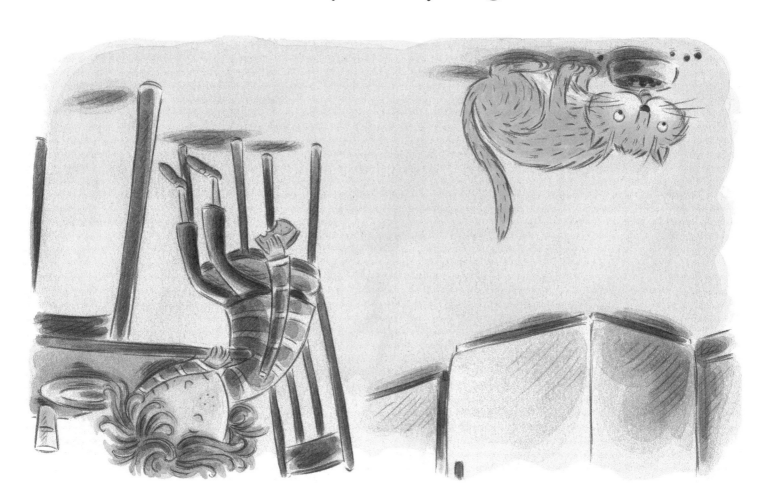

Cat is eating.

5

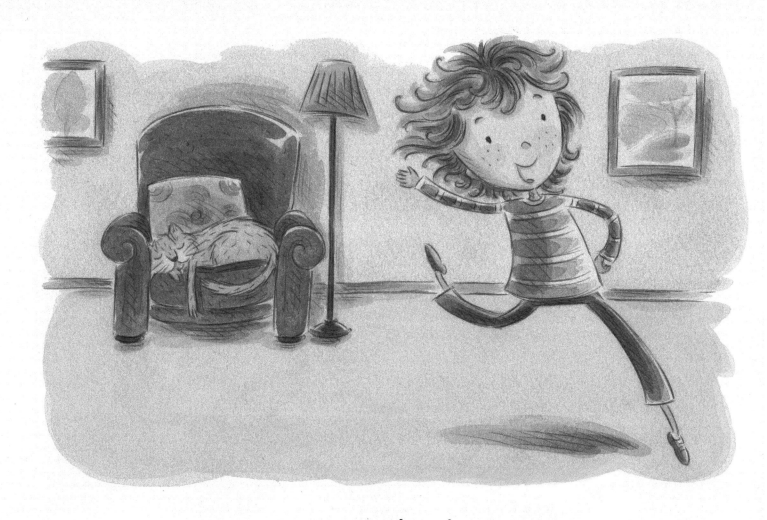

I am playing.

Cat is playing.

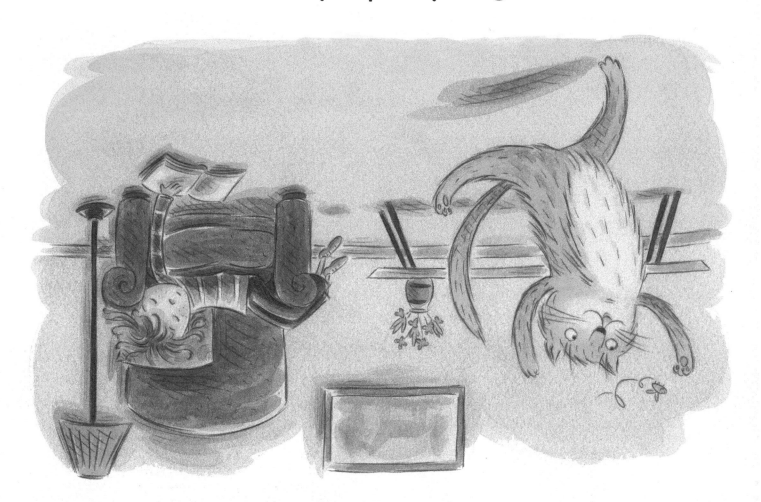

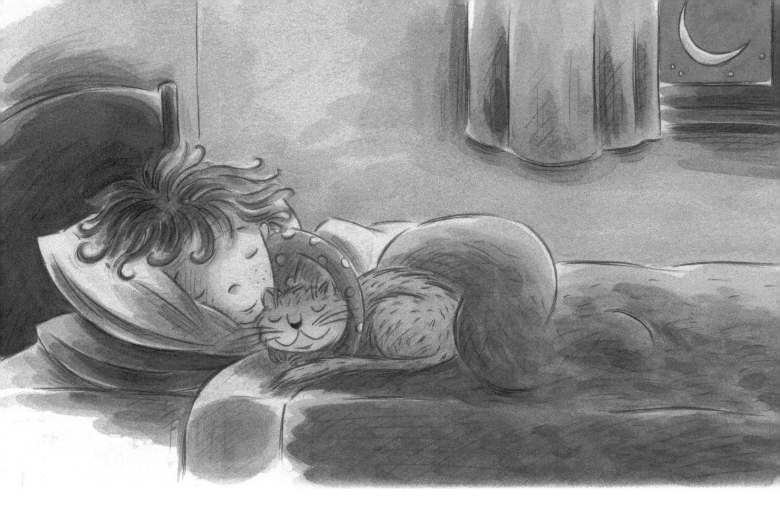

I am sleeping. Cat is sleeping too!